Sugar-Free Desserts

Naturally Sweetened with Fruits & Juices

PUBLICATIONS INTERNATIONAL, LTD.

Photography by Burke/Triolo Productions, Los Angeles, California.
Photographer: Jeff Burke
Photo/Food Stylist: Lorraine Triolo

Recipe development: Karen A. Levin

Recipe analysis and diabetic exchange information by Hill Nutrition Associates, Inc.

Pictured on front cover: Fabulous Fruit Tart (*page 50*).

Pictured on back cover (*clockwise from top right*): Profiteroles with Apricot Pastry Cream (*page 82*); Blueberry-Sour Cream Corn Muffins (*page 6*); Honeydew Ice, Cantaloupe Ice and Watermelon Ice (*page 72*).

Manufactured in U.S.A.

Sugar-Free Desserts

◆

Naturally Sweetened with Fruits & Juices

Sacrifice No More

Looking for a surefire way to satisfy your sweet tooth without the use of refined sugar, molasses, honey or artificial sweeteners? If certain diet restrictions require you or a family member to reduce or eliminate your sugar intake, you are probably well aware of how difficult it is to find good-tasting sugar-free desserts. After experimenting with dissatisfying facsimiles of the "real thing," you may have resigned yourself to a life of sacrifice...no more luscious cakes, creamy pies or other fanciful creations.

Well, sacrifice no more! SUGAR-FREE DESSERTS provides you with dozens of scrumptious easy-to-make recipes that will appeal to not only the person with the dietary restriction but to other family members as well. Page through this unbeatable recipe collection for such classics as Carrot-Pineapple Cake, Fabulous Fruit Tart or fruit-filled Berry Shortcakes. Discover how each of these desserts is sweetened the pure and natural way–with frozen fruit juice concentrates, all-fruit spreads and other healthy alternatives to refined sugar.

Ingredient Information

Fruit Juice Concentrates
When using frozen fruit juice concentrates, be sure to use only the unsweetened varieties. Just measure out what is needed and return the unused portion to the freezer until ready to use again.

All-Fruit Spreads
All-fruit spreads, or spreadable fruits, are a fairly new entry to the supermarket shelves. They are usually found with the fruit jams, jellies and preserves. Available in a wide array of flavors, each sugar-free variety offers the sweetness of all-natural fruit in a convenient form.

Pourable Fruits
Pourable fruits are very similar to all-fruit spreads. However, as the name implies, this product is in a liquid state making it ideal for recipe use as well as serving as a substitute for high-sugar syrups and sauces. Look for pourable

fruits next to the pancake syrup section of your supermarket. Due to its limited distribution, most recipes calling for this product include a quick and easy substitution.

Nutrition and Diet

While it may be your goal to monitor the amount of sugar in your diet, it is equally important to be aware of other dietary information. As an added plus, we have included with each recipe nutrition information as well as diabetic exchange information. The easy-to-read chart following each recipe provides per serving information for calories, protein, carbohydrates, fat, cholesterol and sodium.

Nutrient Information

The analysis of each recipe includes all the ingredients that are listed in that recipe, except ingredients that are labeled as "optional." If a range is offered for an ingredient (2 to 3 teaspoons, for example) the first amount given was used to calculate the nutrition information. If an ingredient is presented with an option (2 teaspoons butter or margarine), the first item listed was used to calculate the nutrition information. Foods shown in photographs on the same serving plate and offered as "serve with" suggestions at the end of the recipe are also not included with the recipe analysis unless it is stated in the per serving line. And finally, only the main recipes, not the variations, have been analyzed. Every effort has been made to check the accuracy of these numbers. However, because numerous variables account for a wide range of values for certain foods, all nutritive analyses that appear in this publication should be considered approximate.

Diabetic Exchange Information

If you are a diabetic, you probably have met with a dietician to work out a meal plan for your specific diet needs. This meal plan is your guide to follow when choosing the number of food choices or exchanges for a single meal or snack. Each meal plan is comprised of six exchange lists–starch/bread, meat and meat substitutes, vegetables, fruit, milk and fat. In these lists, similar foods are grouped together, with every food on the list containing approximately the same amount of carbohydrates, protein, fat and calories. In the amounts given, all the choices on each list are equal. Consequently, any food on a list can be exchanged with any other food item on the same list. Using the exchange lists and following your meal plan will provide you with a wide variety of food choices, and will help distribute calories, carbohydrates, proteins and fats throughout the day to help balance your insulin level. This balance is what gives you good blood-glucose control. **Consult your doctor or dietician for further explanation of how the diabetic exchange information given with these recipes fits the parameters of your specific meal plan.**

It is our hope that SUGAR-FREE DESSERTS can provide you with great-tasting desserts ideal for not just the person on the sugar-restricted diet but the entire family as well. And since beautiful full-page photographs are included with many of the recipes, paging through this publication is almost as satisfying as the end result. Enjoy!

The Bread Basket

BLUEBERRY–SOUR CREAM CORN MUFFINS

1 cup all-purpose flour
¾ cup corn meal
2 teaspoons baking powder
½ teaspoon baking soda
¼ teaspoon salt
1 egg, beaten
1 cup sour cream
⅓ cup thawed frozen unsweetened apple juice concentrate

1½ cups fresh *or* frozen (not thawed) blueberries
⅔ cup whipped cream cheese
2 tablespoons no-sugar-added blueberry fruit spread

Preheat oven to 400°F. Grease twelve medium-sized muffin cups or line with paper liners; set aside. Combine dry ingredients in medium bowl. Add combined egg, sour cream and apple juice concentrate; mix just until dry ingredients are moistened. Gently stir in blueberries. Spoon batter into prepared cups, filling each cup ¾ full. Bake 18 to 20 minutes or until golden brown. Let stand in pan on wire rack 5 minutes. Remove from pan; cool slightly. Combine cream cheese and fruit spread; serve with warm muffins. *Makes 1 dozen*

Nutrients Per Muffin:					
Calories	176	Carbohydrates	23g	Cholesterol	35mg
Protein	4g	Fat	8g	Sodium	201mg
Diabetic Exchanges Per Muffin:					
1 Starch/Bread, 1½ Fat, ½ Fruit					

Blueberry-Sour Cream Corn Muffins

ENGLISH–STYLE SCONES

3 eggs, divided
½ cup heavy cream
1½ teaspoons vanilla
2 cups all-purpose flour
2 teaspoons baking powder
¼ teaspoon salt
¼ cup cold butter or
   margarine
¼ cup finely chopped pitted
   dates

¼ cup golden raisins *or*
   currants
1 teaspoon water
6 tablespoons no-sugar-
   added orange
   marmalade fruit spread
6 tablespoons softly
   whipped cream *or*
   crème fraîche

Preheat oven to 375°F. Beat two eggs with cream and vanilla; set aside. Combine flour, baking powder and salt in medium bowl. Cut in butter with pastry blender or two knives until mixture resembles coarse crumbs. Stir in dates and raisins. Add egg mixture; mix just until dry ingredients are moistened. With floured hands, knead dough four times on lightly floured surface. Place dough on greased cookie sheet; pat into 8-inch circle. With sharp wet knife, gently score dough into six wedges, cutting ¾ of the way into dough. Beat remaining egg with water; brush lightly over dough. Bake 18 to 20 minutes or until golden brown. Cool 5 minutes on wire rack. Cut into wedges. Serve warm with marmalade and whipped cream.   *Makes 6 scones*

Nutrients Per Scone:

Calories	436	Carbohydrates	54g	Cholesterol	164mg
Protein	8g	Fat	21g	Sodium	354mg

Diabetic Exchanges Per Scone:
2¼ Bread, 4 Fat, 1¼ Fruit

APPLE–WALNUT MUFFINS

2 cups all-purpose flour
2 teaspoons baking powder
1½ teaspoons ground
    cinnamon
¼ teaspoon ground nutmeg
¼ teaspoon salt
2 eggs, beaten
⅔ cup thawed frozen
    unsweetened apple
    juice concentrate

⅓ cup butter or margarine,
    melted
1 teaspoon vanilla
1 cup finely chopped,
    peeled apple (about 2
    medium apples)
½ cup chopped walnuts

Preheat oven to 350°F. Grease twelve medium-sized muffin cups or line with paper liners; set aside. Combine dry ingredients in medium bowl. Add combined eggs, apple juice concentrate, butter and vanilla; mix just until dry ingredients are moistened. Stir in apple and walnuts. Spoon batter into prepared cups, filling each cup ¾ full. Bake 25 minutes or until golden brown. Let stand in pan on wire rack 5 minutes. Remove from pan; cool. Serve warm or at room temperature.

Makes 1 dozen

Note: Cooled muffins may be wrapped securely and frozen up to 3 months.

Nutrients Per Muffin:					
Calories	199	Carbohydrates	25g	Cholesterol	49mg
Protein	4g	Fat	9g	Sodium	183g

Diabetic Exchanges Per Muffin:
¼ Starch/Bread, 1¾ Fat, ½ Fruit

APPLE BUTTER

1 jar (23 ounces)
    unsweetened
    applesauce (2½ cups)
½ cup thawed frozen
    unsweetened apple
    juice concentrate

1 teaspoon ground
    cinnamon
½ teaspoon salt
½ teaspoon ground cloves
⅛ teaspoon ground allspice

Combine all ingredients in heavy medium saucepan. Cook over medium heat 50 minutes or until very thick, stirring occasionally. Store in sealed container in refrigerator up to 3 weeks. Spread on toast or muffins.

Makes 2 cups

Nutrients Per Tablespoon:						
Calories	16	Carbohydrates	4mg	Cholesterol	0mg
Protein	tr	Fat	tr	Sodium	36mg
Diabetic Exchanges Per Tablespoon:						
¼ Fruit						

ORANGE MUFFINS

2 cups all-purpose flour
2 teaspoons baking powder
½ teaspoon baking soda
¼ teaspoon salt
1 tablespoon grated orange peel
1 egg, beaten
¾ cup orange juice

¼ cup butter or margarine, melted
2 tablespoons milk
1 teaspoon vanilla
Whipped butter (optional)
No-sugar-added orange marmalade fruit spread (optional)

Preheat oven to 400°F. Grease twelve medium-sized muffin cups or line with paper liners; set aside. Combine dry ingredients and orange peel in medium bowl. Add combined egg, orange juice, butter, milk and vanilla; mix just until dry ingredients are moistened. Spoon batter into prepared muffin cups, filling each cup ½ full. Bake 18 to 20 minutes or until golden brown. Let cool in pan on wire rack 5 minutes. Remove from pan; cool. Serve warm or at room temperature. Spread with whipped butter and marmalade, if desired.

Makes 1 dozen

Nutrients Per Muffin:						
Calories	127	Carbohydrates	18g	Cholesterol	28mg
Protein	3g	Fat	5g	Sodium	196mg
Diabetic Exchanges Per Muffin:						
1 Starch/Bread, 1 Fat						

PEANUT BUTTER & JAM MUFFINS

2 cups all-purpose flour
2 teaspoons baking powder
1 teaspoon baking soda
2 eggs
½ cup no-sugar-added natural peanut butter
¾ cup thawed frozen unsweetened apple juice concentrate

¼ cup milk
¼ cup butter or margarine, melted
½ cup chopped salted peanuts
6 tablespoons no-sugar-added strawberry fruit spread

Preheat oven to 350°F. Grease twelve medium-sized muffin cups or line with paper liners; set aside. Combine dry ingredients in medium bowl; set aside. Beat together eggs and peanut butter in separate medium bowl until smooth. Blend in apple juice concentrate, milk and butter. Add to dry ingredients; mix just until dry ingredients are moistened. Stir in peanuts. Spoon half of batter evenly into prepared muffin cups. Drop 1½ teaspoons strawberry fruit spread into center of each cup; cover with remaining batter. Bake 18 minutes or until golden brown. Let stand in pan on wire rack 5 minutes. Remove from pan; cool. Serve warm or at room temperature. *Makes 1 dozen*

Nutrients Per Muffin:

Calories	278	Carbohydrates	32g	Cholesterol	46mg
Protein	8g	Fat	13g	Sodium	288mg

Diabetic Exchanges Per Muffin:
1¼ Starch/Bread, ½ High-Fat Meat, 2 Fat, ¾ Fruit,

Peanut Butter & Jam Muffins

COCONUT DATE NUT QUICK BREAD

2 cups all-purpose flour
2 teaspoons baking powder
½ teaspoon baking soda
½ teaspoon salt
2 eggs
¾ cup thawed frozen
    unsweetened apple
    juice concentrate
¼ cup butter or margarine,
    melted

¼ cup milk
2 teaspoons vanilla
1 cup chopped pitted dates
½ cup chopped walnuts *or*
    pecans
⅓ cup unsweetened flaked
    coconut*
Cream cheese (optional)

Preheat oven to 350°F. Combine dry ingredients in medium bowl; set aside. Beat eggs in separate medium bowl. Blend in apple juice concentrate, butter, milk and vanilla. Add to dry ingredients; mix just until moistened. Stir in dates, walnuts and coconut. Spread into greased 9 × 5-inch loaf pan. Bake 45 minutes or until wooden pick inserted in center comes out clean. Cool 10 minutes in pan on wire rack. Remove from pan; cool completely. Slice and serve at room temperature, or toast slices and spread with cream cheese, if desired.

Makes 12 servings

Unsweetened flaked coconut is available in health food stores.

Nutrients Per Serving:					
Calories	242	Carbohydrates	36g	Cholesterol	46mg
Protein	5g	Fat	9g	Sodium	255mg

Diabetic Exchanges Per Serving:
1¼ Starch/Bread, 1¾ Fat, 1¼ Fruit

Coconut Date Nut Quick Bread

Luscious Cakes

STRAWBERRY CHEESECAKE

3 packages (8 ounces *each*)
cream cheese, softened
1 cup no-sugar-added
strawberry pourable
fruit*
3 teaspoons vanilla, divided

¼ teaspoon salt
4 eggs
1 cup sour cream** *or* creme
fraiche
Fresh strawberry halves
or slices (optional)

Preheat oven to 325°F. Beat cream cheese in large bowl until creamy.
Blend in pourable fruit, 1 teaspoon vanilla and salt. Add eggs, one at
a time, beating well after each addition. Pour into greased 9-inch
springform pan. Bake 50 minutes. Combine sour cream and remaining
2 teaspoons vanilla; mix well. Carefully spoon over warm cheesecake.
Return to oven; continue baking 10 minutes or just until set. Turn
oven off; leave cheesecake in oven, with door closed, 30 minutes.
Transfer to wire rack; loosen cheesecake from rim of pan. Cool
completely before removing rim. Cover and chill at least 6 hours or
overnight. Just before serving, garnish cheesecake with strawberries, if
desired.   *Makes 10 servings*

*¾ cup no-sugar-added strawberry fruit spread combined with ¼ cup
warm water may be substituted.*

**Do not use reduced-calorie sour cream.*

Nutrients Per Serving:

Calories	379	Carbohydrates	18g	Cholesterol	170mg
Protein	8g	Fat	31g	Sodium	313mg

Diabetic Exchanges Per Serving:
1 Medium-Fat Meat, 5 Fat, 1¼ Fruit

PEACH MELBA LAYER CAKE SUPREME

2 cups all-purpose flour
2 teaspoons baking powder
¼ teaspoon salt
½ cup butter or margarine, softened
3 egg yolks
1 teaspoon vanilla
1 cup thawed frozen unsweetened apple juice concentrate
1 can (16 ounces) sliced peaches in unsweetened juice, drained, *or* 1½ cups thawed frozen unsweetened sliced peaches

2 cups fresh *or* thawed frozen unsweetened raspberries
⅓ cup no-sugar-added peach pourable fruit*
⅓ cup no-sugar-added seedless raspberry fruit spread

Preheat oven to 375°F. Grease and flour two 8-inch round cake pans. Combine flour, baking powder and salt; set aside. Beat butter at medium speed in large bowl of electric mixer until light and fluffy. Blend in egg yolks and vanilla. Alternately add dry ingredients and apple juice concentrate, beating well after each addition; spread evenly into prepared pans. Bake 20 minutes or until golden brown and wooden pick inserted in centers comes out clean. Cool 10 minutes in pans on wire racks. Remove from pans; cool completely.

Drain peaches. Combine with raspberries and pourable fruit; mix lightly. Spread fruit spread evenly over one cake layer; top with second cake layer. Spoon fruit mixture over top of cake, letting excess fruit mixture drip down sides. *Makes 8 servings*

* 3 tablespoons no-sugar-added peach spread combined with 2 tablespoons warm water may be substituted.

Nutrients Per Serving:					
Calories	390	Carbohydrates	62g	Cholesterol	111mg
Protein	5g	Fat	14g	Sodium	314mg
Diabetic Exchanges Per Serving:					
1½ Starch/Bread, 3 Fat, 2½ Fruit					

Peach Melba Layer Cake Supreme

FRUIT & NUT COFFEECAKE RING

1 package active dry yeast
½ cup warm water (115°F)
4 cups all-purpose flour, divided
1 teaspoon salt
1 teaspoon ground cardamom (optional)
⅓ cup butter or margarine, melted
⅓ cup thawed frozen unsweetened apple juice concentrate

3 eggs, divided
½ cup no-sugar-added apricot fruit spread
1 package (6 ounces) mixed dried fruit, chopped
½ cup coarsely chopped toasted pecans
1 teaspoon cold water

Dissolve yeast in warm water; let stand 10 minutes. In large bowl of electric mixer, combine 3 cups flour, salt and cardamom, if desired. While mixing on low speed with dough hook, gradually blend in yeast mixture, butter, apple juice concentrate and two eggs. Beat 2 minutes at medium speed. Beat in enough remaining flour to form a stiff dough. Continue to beat until dough is smooth and elastic.* Let rest 20 minutes. Roll out dough on lightly floured surface to 22 × 12-inch rectangle. Spread fruit spread evenly down center of rectangle, leaving 1 inch border along both long sides. Sprinkle fruit bits and nuts evenly over fruit spread. Starting at one long side, roll dough up tightly; pinch seam to seal. Place on greased cookie sheet. Bring ends of roll together to form ring; pinch ends together to seal, using water if necessary. With scissors or sharp knife, make diagonal cuts, about 1 inch apart, into top of ring. Let rise in warm place 30 minutes. (Dough will not double in volume.)

Preheat oven to 375°F. Beat together remaining egg and cold water; brush over ring. Bake 25 to 30 minutes or until golden brown. Immediately remove from pan. Cool on wire rack. Serve warm or at room temperature. *Makes 10 servings*

Dough may be kneaded by hand on lightly floured surface until smooth and elastic, about 10 minutes.

Nutrients Per Serving:					
Calories	386	Carbohydrates	64g	Cholesterol	80mg
Protein	8g	Fat	12g	Sodium	308mg

Diabetic Exchanges Per Serving:
2¼ Starch/Bread, 2¼ Fat, 2 Fruit

Fruit & Nut Coffeecake Ring

BERRY SHORTCAKES

1¾ cups all-purpose flour
1 tablespoon baking
   powder
⅛ teaspoon salt
½ cup cold butter or
   margarine
½ cup milk
1 teaspoon vanilla
1 egg
1 teaspoon water

1 cup sliced strawberries
1 cup raspberries
1 cup blueberries
3 tablespoons no-sugar-
   added strawberry
   pourable fruit*
4 tablespoons almond-
   flavored liqueur,**
   divided
1 cup heavy cream

Preheat oven to 425°F. Combine flour, baking powder and salt in medium bowl. Cut in butter with pastry blender or two knives until mixture resembles coarse crumbs. Add milk and vanilla; mix just until dry ingredients are moistened. Knead dough gently on lightly floured surface ten times. Roll or pat out to ½-inch thickness. Cut with 3-inch heart- or round-shaped biscuit cutter; place on ungreased cookie sheet. If necessary, reroll scraps of dough in order to make six shortcakes. Beat together egg and water; brush lightly over dough. Bake 12 to 14 minutes or until golden brown. Cool slightly on wire rack.

While shortcakes are baking, combine berries, pourable fruit and 3 tablespoons liqueur; let stand at room temperature 15 minutes. Beat cream with remaining 1 tablespoon liqueur until soft peaks form. Split warm shortcakes; fill with about ⅔ of the berry and whipped cream mixtures. Replace tops of shortcakes; top with remaining berry and whipped cream mixtures. *Makes 6 servings*

2 tablespoons no-sugar-added strawberry fruit spread combined with 1 tablespoon warm water may be substituted.

**3 tablespoons thawed frozen unsweetened apple juice concentrate plus ½ teaspoon almond extract may be substituted for the liqueur in the berry mixture, and 1 tablespoon thawed frozen unsweetened apple juice concentrate may be substituted for the liqueur in the whipped cream mixture.*

Nutrients Per Serving:

| Calories | 511 | Carbohydrates | 46g | Cholesterol | 134mg |
| Protein | 7g | Fat | 32g | Sodium | 460mg |

Diabetic Exchanges Per Serving:
2 Starch/Bread, 6⅓ Fat, 1 Fruit

Berry Shortcake

BANANA–NUT CAKE

2¼ cups all-purpose flour
¾ cup uncooked rolled oats
2 teaspoons ground cinnamon
2 teaspoons baking powder
1 teaspoon baking soda
¼ teaspoon salt
2 cups mashed ripe bananas (about 6 medium bananas)
¾ cup thawed frozen unsweetened apple juice concentrate
4 eggs, beaten
½ cup butter or margarine, melted
2 teaspoons vanilla
¾ cup chopped walnuts
Cream Cheese Glaze (recipe follows)

Preheat oven to 350°F. Combine dry ingredients in large bowl. Add all remaining ingredients *except* walnuts and Cream Cheese Glaze; mix well. Stir in walnuts; spread into well-greased Bundt or tube pan. Bake 50 to 55 minutes or until wooden pick inserted in center comes out clean. Cool in pan on wire rack 15 minutes; turn cake out onto wire rack. Cool completely. If desired, prepare Cream Cheese Glaze. Spoon over top of cake, letting excess glaze drip down sides. Serve at room temperature or chilled.   *Makes 12 servings*

CREAM CHEESE GLAZE

3 ounces regular *or* reduced calorie cream cheese, softened
2 tablespoons thawed frozen unsweetened apple juice concentrate
¼ teaspoon vanilla
⅛ teaspoon ground cinnamon

Combine all ingredients in small bowl; beat until smooth.

Nutrients Per Serving:					
Calories	313	Carbohydrates	40g	Cholesterol	92mg
Protein	7g	Fat	15g	Sodium	290mg
Diabetic Exchanges Per Serving:					
1½ Starch/Bread, 3 Fat, 1 Fruit					

Banana-Nut Cake

RASPBERRY–ALMOND LAYER CAKE

3 egg yolks
1 cup thawed frozen
    unsweetened apple
    juice concentrate
¾ cup butter or margarine,
    melted and cooled
1 teaspoon almond extract
2½ cups all-purpose flour
2 teaspoons baking powder
¼ teaspoon salt
⅓ cup chopped toasted
    almonds
4 egg whites

¼ teaspoon cream of tartar
1 cup heavy cream
½ cup no-sugar-added
    seedless raspberry fruit
    spread
2 tablespoons almond-
    flavored liqueur
    (optional)
⅓ cup toasted slivered
    almonds
    Fresh raspberries
    (optional)

Preheat oven to 350°F. Grease and flour two (9-inch) round cake pans; set aside. Beat egg yolks in large bowl. Blend in apple juice concentrate, butter and extract. Combine flour, baking powder and salt. Gradually add to egg yolk mixture, beating until well blended. Stir in chopped almonds. Beat egg whites with cream of tartar at high speed in small bowl of electric mixer until stiff peaks form. Gently fold into batter; spread evenly into prepared pans. Bake 18 to 20 minutes or until cake is golden brown around edges. Cool in pans on wire racks 10 minutes. Invert cakes onto racks; remove pans. Cool completely.

Beat cream at high speed in small bowl of electric mixer until soft peaks form. Add fruit spread, 1 tablespoon at a time, beating until thick and well blended. Brush liqueur evenly over cake layers; stack layers. Frost top and sides with whipped cream mixture; press slivered almonds around edge. Garnish with fresh raspberries, if desired.

Makes 8 servings

Nutrients Per Serving:

| Calories | 595 | Carbohydrates | 59g | Cholesterol | 167mg |
| Protein | 10g | Fat | 36g | Sodium | 402mg |

Diabetic Exchanges Per Serving:
2 Starch/Bread, 7 Fat, 1¾ Fruit

Raspberry-Almond Layer Cake

BRAIDED ORANGE–CURRANT COFFEECAKE

3 cups all-purpose flour,
   divided
¾ teaspoon salt
1 package quick-rise yeast
1 cup unsweetened orange
   juice
1 tablespoon butter or
   margarine, melted
1 teaspoon grated orange
   peel

½ cup currants *or* chopped
   raisins
1 egg
1 teaspoon cold water
   Whipped butter (optional)
   No-sugar-added orange
   marmalade fruit spread
   (optional)

Combine 2 cups flour, salt and yeast in large bowl of electric mixer. Heat orange juice to 130°F. Add to flour mixture along with butter and orange peel. Beat on medium speed with electric mixer fitted with dough hook.* Add only enough of the remaining 1 cup flour to make a soft dough; continue to beat dough until smooth and elastic, about 3 minutes. Transfer to lightly floured surface; knead in currants. Roll out dough to 13 × 6-inch rectangle. Starting at one short end, cut dough lengthwise into three equal strips, leaving dough attached 1 inch from opposite short end. Braid strips together; press braided ends together to seal. Place on greased cookie sheet; cover with greased waxed paper. Let rise in warm place until doubled in volume, about 20 minutes.

Preheat oven to 450°F. Bake coffeecake 13 minutes. Beat egg with water; brush over coffeecake. Return coffeecake to oven; continue baking 3 to 5 minutes or until deep golden brown. Cool on wire rack. Serve warm or at room temperature with butter and marmalade, if desired. *Makes 6 servings*

Dough may also be kneaded by hand on lightly floured surface until smooth and elastic, about 10 minutes.

Note: Leftover coffeecake may be sliced, toasted and served with whipped cream cheese *or* made into French toast and served with no-sugar-added pourable fruit.

Nutrients Per Serving:					
Calories	313	Carbohydrates	62g	Cholesterol	41mg
Protein	9g	Fat	3g	Sodium	308mg
Diabetic Exchanges Per Serving:					
3¼ Starch/Bread, ⅔ Fat, ½ Fruit					

Braided Orange-Currant Coffeecake

CARROT–PINEAPPLE CAKE

½ cup butter or margarine,
  softened
3 eggs
1 cup thawed frozen
  unsweetened pineapple
  juice concentrate
2 teaspoons vanilla
2½ cups all-purpose flour
2 teaspoons baking powder
1 teaspoon baking soda
1 teaspoon ground nutmeg
1 teaspoon ground
  cinnamon
¼ teaspoon salt
3 cups shredded carrots
  Icing (recipe follows)
½ cup chopped toasted
  pecans (optional)

Preheat oven to 350°F. Beat butter in large bowl until creamy. Blend in eggs, pineapple juice concentrate and vanilla. Combine flour, baking powder, baking soda, spices and salt. Gradually add to egg mixture, beating until well blended. Stir in carrots. Spread batter evenly into greased 12 × 8-inch baking dish. Bake 30 minutes or until wooden pick inserted in center comes out clean. Cool completely on wire rack. Prepare Icing; spread over cooled cake. Sprinkle with pecans, if desired. *Makes 12 servings*

ICING

1 package (8 ounces) cream
  cheese, softened
1 can (8 ounces) crushed
  pineapple in
  unsweetened juice, well
  drained
1 teaspoon vanilla

Combine all ingredients; mix well.

Nutrients Per Serving:					
Calories	319	Carbohydrates	37g	Cholesterol	95mg
Protein	6g	Fat	16g	Sodium	346mg
Diabetic Exchanges Per Serving:					
1½ Starch/Bread, 3 Fat, 1 Fruit					

Carrot-Pineapple Cake

SNACKING APPLESAUCE CAKE SQUARES

⅓ cup butter or margarine, softened
2 eggs
⅔ cup thawed frozen unsweetened apple juice concentrate
½ cup unsweetened applesauce
2 cups all-purpose flour

2 teaspoons baking powder
2 teaspoons ground cinnamon
½ teaspoon baking soda
¼ teaspoon salt
1 large cooking apple, peeled and chopped
Creamy Topping (recipe follows), optional

Preheat oven to 375°F. Beat butter in large bowl until creamy. Blend in eggs, apple juice concentrate and applesauce. Combine dry ingredients. Gradually add to egg mixture, beating until well blended. Stir in apple. Spread batter evenly into greased 8- or 9-inch square baking pan. Bake 20 to 25 minutes or until wooden pick inserted in center comes out clean. Cool on wire rack. Cut into squares; serve warm or at room temperature with Creamy Topping, if desired.

Makes 9 servings

CREAMY TOPPING

½ cup heavy cream
1 teaspoon vanilla

¼ teaspoon ground cinnamon

Beat cream in small bowl at high speed of electric mixer until soft peaks form. Beat in vanilla and cinnamon until stiff peaks form.

Nutrients Per Serving:					
Calories	229	Carbohydrates	34g	Cholesterol	65mg
Protein	4g	Fat	8g	Sodium	209mg

Diabetic Exchanges Per Serving:
1¼ Starch/Bread, 1¾ Fat, 1 Fruit

POPPYSEED CAKE

2 eggs, beaten
½ cup thawed frozen unsweetened apple juice concentrate
⅓ cup butter or margarine, melted
1 tablespoon grated lemon peel

1 tablespoon fresh lemon juice
1 teaspoon vanilla
1 cup all-purpose flour
⅓ cup poppy seeds
1½ teaspoons baking powder
½ teaspoon baking soda
⅛ teaspoon salt

Preheat oven to 350°F. Beat eggs in large bowl. Blend in apple juice concentrate, butter, lemon peel, lemon juice and vanilla. Combine flour, poppy seeds, baking powder, baking soda and salt. Gradually add to egg mixture, beating until well blended. Pour batter into greased 9-inch square baking pan. Bake 20 minutes or until wooden pick inserted in center comes out clean and edges are golden brown. Cool on wire rack. Serve warm or at room temperature.

Makes 8 servings

Nutrients Per Serving:

Calories	206	Carbohydrates	21g	Cholesterol	74mg
Protein	4g	Fat	12g	Sodium	265mg

Diabetic Exchanges Per Serving:
1 Startch/Bread, ¼ Medium-Fat Meat, 2 Fat, ½ Fruit

PINEAPPLE UPSIDE–DOWN CAKE

¼ **cup *plus* 2 tablespoons butter or margarine, melted, divided**
½ **teaspoon ground cinnamon**
1 **can (8 ounces) pineapple rings in unsweetened juice, drained**
Frozen unsweetened dark cherries, thawed

2 **eggs**
½ **cup no-sugar-added pineapple fruit spread**
1 **cup buttermilk**
1½ **cups all-purpose flour**
1 **teaspoon baking powder**
½ **teaspoon baking soda**
¼ **teaspoon salt**

Preheat oven to 350°F. Combine 2 tablespoons melted butter and cinnamon; mix well. Spread onto bottom of 8-inch square baking dish. Top with pineapple rings; place cherries in centers of rings. Beat eggs in medium bowl; blend in remaining butter, fruit spread and buttermilk. Combine flour, baking powder, soda and salt. Gradually add to buttermilk mixture, beating until well blended. Spread batter evenly over fruit. Bake 30 minutes or until wooden pick inserted in center comes out clean. Cool in baking dish on wire rack 30 minutes. Invert onto serving platter; remove dish. Serve warm or at room temperature.

Makes 6 servings

Nutrients Per Serving:

Calories	339	Carbohydrates	47g	Cholesterol	104mg
Protein	7g	Fat	14g	Sodium	411mg

Diabetic Exchanges Per Serving:
1½ Starch/Bread, 2¼ Fat, 1½ Fruit

Cookie Sampler

MACADAMIA NUT CRUNCHIES

1 egg, beaten
½ cup mashed ripe banana
  (about 2 medium
  bananas)
⅓ cup butter or margarine,
  melted
¼ cup no-sugar-added
  pineapple fruit spread
1 teaspoon vanilla

1¼ cups all-purpose flour
⅓ cup unsweetened flaked
  coconut*
½ teaspoon baking powder
½ teaspoon salt
1 jar (3½ ounces)
  macadamia nuts,
  coarsely chopped
  (about ¾ cup)

Preheat oven to 375°F. Combine egg, banana, butter, fruit spread and vanilla in medium bowl. Add flour, coconut, baking powder and salt; mix well. Stir in nuts. Drop tablespoonfuls of dough, 2 inches apart, onto lightly greased cookie sheets. Bake 10 to 12 minutes or until lightly browned. Cool on wire racks. Store in tightly covered container.   *Makes 2 dozen*

Unsweetened flaked coconut is available in health food stores.

Nutrients Per Cookie:					
Calories	96	Carbohydrates	9g	Cholesterol	16mg
Protein	1g	Fat	6g	Sodium	83mg
Diabetic Exchanges Per Cookie:					
⅓ Starch/Bread, 1¼ Fat, ¼ Fruit					

Macadamia Nut Crunchies

KOLACKY

½ cup butter or margarine,
  softened
3 ounces regular *or* reduced
  calorie cream cheese,
  softened
1 teaspoon vanilla
1 cup all-purpose flour

⅛ teaspoon salt
6 teaspoons no-sugar-added
  fruit spread, assorted
  flavors
1 egg
1 teaspoon cold water

Combine butter and cream cheese in large bowl; beat until smooth and creamy. Blend in vanilla. Combine flour and salt; gradually add to butter mixture, mixing until mixture forms soft dough. Divide dough in half; wrap each half in plastic wrap. Refrigerate until firm.

Preheat oven to 375°F. Roll out half of dough on lightly floured pastry cloth or board to ⅛-inch thickness. Cut with top of glass or biscuit cutter into 3-inch rounds. Spoon ½ teaspoon fruit spread onto center of each dough circle. Beat egg with water; lightly brush onto edges of dough circles. Bring three edges of dough up over fruit spread; pinch edges together to seal. Place on ungreased cookie sheets; brush with egg mixture. Repeat with remaining dough and fruit spread. Bake 12 minutes or until golden brown. Let stand on cookie sheets 1 minute; transfer to wire rack. Cool completely. Store in tightly covered container.

Makes 2 dozen

Nutrients Per Kolacky:					
Calories	76	Carbohydrates	6g	Cholesterol	23mg
Protein	1g	Fat	5g	Sodium	64mg

Diabetic Exchanges Per Kolacky:
⅓ Starch/Bread, 1 Fat

APRICOT BARS

2 eggs
1 cup no-sugar-added
  apricot fruit spread
½ cup butter or margarine,
  melted
2 teaspoons vanilla
1 cup all-purpose flour

⅔ cup uncooked rolled oats
1¼ teaspoons baking powder
¼ teaspoon salt
¾ teaspoon ground
  cinnamon
¼ teaspoon allspice
⅛ teaspoon mace

continued on page 38

Apricot Bars, continued

Preheat oven to 350°F. Beat eggs in large bowl. Blend in fruit spread, butter and vanilla. Add flour, oats, baking powder, salt and spices; mix well. Spread dough into greased 12 × 8-inch baking dish. Bake 18 minutes or until golden brown and firm to the touch. Cool completely on wire rack. Cut into bars. Store in tightly covered container.

Makes 1½ dozen

Nutrients Per Bar:					
Calories	130	Carbohydrates	17g	Cholesterol	37mg
Protein	2g	Fat	6g	Sodium	119mg
Diabetic Exchanges Per Bar:					
⅔ Starch/Bread, 1 Fat, ½ Fruit					

PEANUT BUTTER & BANANA COOKIES

¼ cup butter or margarine
½ cup mashed ripe banana (about 2 medium bananas)
½ cup no-sugar-added natural peanut butter
1 egg
¼ cup thawed frozen unsweetened apple juice concentrate
1 teaspoon vanilla
1 cup all-purpose flour
½ teaspoon baking soda
¼ teaspoon salt
½ cup chopped salted peanuts
Whole peanuts (optional)

Preheat oven to 375°F. Beat butter in large bowl until creamy. Add banana and peanut butter; beat until smooth. Blend in egg, apple juice concentrate and vanilla. Beat in flour, baking soda and salt. Stir in chopped peanuts. Drop rounded tablespoonfuls of dough, 2 inches apart, onto lightly greased cookie sheets; top each with one peanut, if desired. Bake 8 minutes or until set. Cool completely on wire rack. Store in tightly covered container.

Makes 2 dozen

Nutrients Per Cookie:					
Calories	100	Carbohydrates	8g	Cholesterol	14mg
Protein	3g	Fat	6g	Sodium	84mg
Diabetic Exchanges Per Cookie:					
¼ Starch/Bread, ¼ High-Fat Meat, 1 Fat, ¼ Fruit					

Peanut Butter & Banana Cookies

LAYERED CUSTARD BARS

1 cup all-purpose flour
⅛ teaspoon salt
½ cup *plus* 1 tablespoon cold butter or margarine, divided
2 tablespoons almond-flavored liqueur *or* 2 tablespoons thawed frozen unsweetened apple juice concentrate *plus* ½ teaspoon almond extract

1 can (16 ounces) sliced peaches *or* apricot halves in unsweetened juice,* well drained
2 eggs, slightly beaten
½ cup no-sugar-added peach *or* apricot pourable fruit**
¼ cup sliced almonds
¼ teaspoon ground cinnamon

Preheat oven to 350°F. Combine flour and salt in medium bowl. Cut in ½ cup butter with pastry blender or two knives until mixture resembles coarse crumbs. Add liqueur; mix well. Press dough evenly onto bottom of 8-inch square baking pan. Bake 15 minutes or until set.

Arrange peaches evenly over partially baked crust. Combine eggs and pourable fruit; mix until well blended. Pour evenly over peaches; set aside. Melt remaining 1 tablespoon butter. Add almonds and cinnamon; mix lightly. Sprinkle almond mixture evenly over egg mixture. Bake 20 to 25 minutes or until almonds are golden brown and custard is set. Cool completely on wire rack. Cut into bars. Serve at room temperature or chilled. Refrigerate leftover bars.

Makes 1 dozen

Cut apricot halves into thirds before placing on crust.

** *6 tablespoons no-sugar-added peach or apricot fruit spread combined with 2 tablespoons warm water may be substituted.*

Nutrients Per Bar:					
Calories	186	Carbohydrates	20g	Cholesterol	59mg
Protein	3g	Fat	20g	Sodium	132mg

Diabetic Exchanges Per Bar:
⅔ Starch/Bread, 2 Fat, ⅔ Fruit

Layered Custard Bars

JUMBO FRUITED OATMEAL COOKIES

¾ cup butter or margarine,
   softened
3 eggs
¾ cup thawed frozen
   unsweetened apple
   juice concentrate
1½ teaspoons vanilla
1½ cups all-purpose flour
1½ cups uncooked rolled oats
½ teaspoon baking soda

½ teaspoon salt
½ teaspoon ground
   cinnamon
½ teaspoon allspice
1 package (6 ounces) dried
   mixed fruit, chopped
   (about 1⅓ cups)
½ cup coarsely chopped
   nuts

Preheat oven to 350°F. Beat butter in large bowl until creamy. Blend in eggs, apple juice concentrate and vanilla. Add flour, oats, baking soda, salt, cinnamon and allspice; mix well. Stir in dried fruit and nuts. Drop scant ¼ cupfuls of dough, 3 inches apart, onto lightly greased cookie sheets; flatten slightly. Bake 12 to 14 minutes or until edges are lightly browned. Cool 1 minute on cookie sheets; transfer to wire rack to cool completely. Store in tightly covered container.

Makes 1½ dozen jumbo cookies

Nutrients Per Cookie:					
Calories	209	Carbohydrates	24g	Cholesterol	56mg
Protein	4g	Fat	11g	Sodium	239mg
Diabetic Exchanges Per Cookie:					
1 Starch/Bread, 2¼ Fat, ½ Fruit					

CHEWY APPLE MOONS

¾ cup thawed frozen
   unsweetened apple
   juice concentrate
½ cup coarsely chopped
   dried apples
2 eggs
¼ cup butter or margarine,
   melted and cooled

1 teaspoon vanilla
1¼ cups all-purpose flour
½ teaspoon baking powder
½ teaspoon ground
   cinnamon
¼ teaspoon salt
⅛ teaspoon ground nutmeg

Preheat oven to 350°F. Combine apple juice concentrate and apples; let stand 10 minutes. Beat eggs in medium bowl. Blend in concentrate mixture, butter and vanilla. Add remaining ingredients; mix well. Drop tablespoonfuls of dough, 2 inches apart, onto greased cookie sheets. Bake 10 to 12 minutes or until firm and golden brown. Cool on wire rack. Store in tightly covered container. *Makes 1½ dozen*

Nutrients Per Cookie:

Calories	89	Carbohydrates	13g	Cholesterol	31mg
Protein	2g	Fat	3g	Sodium	80mg

Diabetic Exchanges Per Cookie:
½ Starch/Bread, ⅔ Fat, ⅓ Fruit

PINEAPPLE–RAISIN BARS

2 eggs
1 cup thawed frozen
    unsweetened pineapple
    juice concentrate
¼ cup butter or margarine,
    melted
1 teaspoon vanilla
1⅓ cups all-purpose flour
⅔ cup uncooked rolled oats
1 teaspoon baking soda
¼ teaspoon salt

1 teaspoon ground
    cinnamon
½ teaspoon ground ginger
⅛ teaspoon ground nutmeg
1 can (8 ounces) crushed
    pineapple in
    unsweetened juice, well
    drained
¾ cup lightly toasted
    chopped pecans
½ cup golden raisins

Preheat oven to 350°F. Beat eggs in large bowl. Blend in pineapple juice concentrate, butter and vanilla. Add flour, oats, baking soda, salt and spices; mix well. Stir in pineapple, pecans and raisins. Spread batter into greased 12 × 8-inch baking dish. Bake 18 to 20 minutes or until firm. Cool completely on wire rack. Cut into bars. Store in tightly covered container. *Makes 16 bars*

Nutrients Per Bar:

Calories	159	Carbohydrates	21g	Cholesterol	34mg
Protein	3g	Fat	7g	Sodium	124mg

Diabetic Exchanges Per Bar:
¾ Starch/Bread, 1½ Fat, ½ Fruit

Pleasin' Pies & Tarts

CHERRY TURNOVERS

8 frozen phyllo dough
   sheets, thawed
¼ cup butter or margarine,
   melted
6 tablespoons no-sugar-
   added black cherry fruit
   spread

1½ tablespoons cherry
   liqueur (optional)
1 egg
1 teaspoon cold water

Preheat oven to 400°F. Lightly brush each phyllo sheet with butter; stack. Cut through all sheets to form six (5-inch) squares. Combine fruit spread and cherry liqueur, if desired. Place 1 tablespoon fruit spread mixture in center of each pile of eight phyllo squares; brush edges of phyllo with butter. Fold edges over to form triangle; gently press edges together to seal. Place on ungreased cookie sheet. Beat together egg and water; brush over phyllo triangles. Bake 10 minutes or until golden brown. Cool on wire rack. Serve warm or at room temperature. *Makes 6 turnovers*

Nutrients Per Turnover:					
Calories	206	Carbohydrates	28g	Cholesterol	56mg
Protein	4g	Fat	9g	Sodium	201mg

Diabetic Exchanges Per Turnover:
1¼ Starch/Bread, 1¾ Fat, ⅔ Fruit

Cherry Turnovers

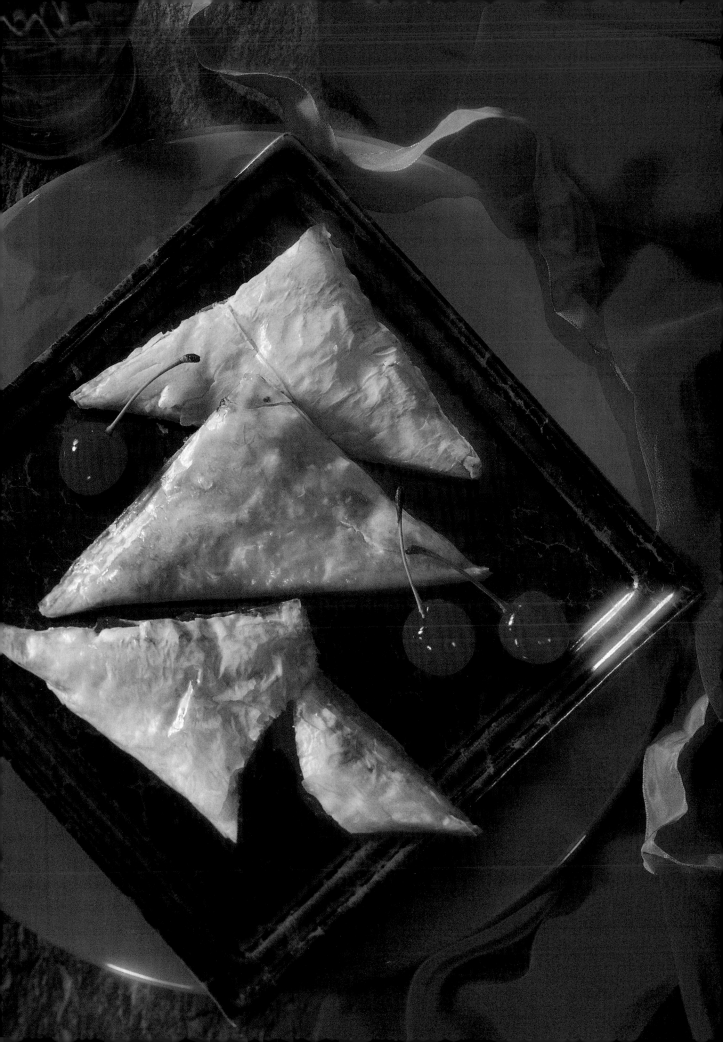

STRAWBERRY RHUBARB PIE

3 cups sliced fresh *or*
   frozen rhubarb, divided
½ cup unsweetened white
   grape juice
2 tablespoons cornstarch
1 teaspoon ground
   cinnamon
¼ teaspoon ground nutmeg
¼ teaspoon salt
1 pint fresh strawberries,
   sliced (about 3½ cups)

¾ cup no-sugar-added
   strawberry fruit spread,
   divided
Pastry for double-crust
   9-inch pie
1 egg yolk, lightly beaten
1 tablespoon sour cream *or*
   milk

Preheat oven to 450°F. Combine 2 cups rhubarb and grape juice in medium saucepan. Bring to a boil over medium heat. Reduce heat to low. Simmer, uncovered, until rhubarb is tender, 8 to 10 minutes for fresh, or 5 minutes for frozen; drain. Combine cornstarch, cinnamon, nutmeg and salt in medium bowl; mix well. Add strawberries; toss to coat. Stir in cooked rhubarb and ½ cup fruit spread. Stir in remaining 1 cup rhubarb. Roll out half of pastry to 11-inch circle; place in 9-inch pie plate. Trim pastry and flute edges, sealing to edge of pie plate. Fill shell with fruit mixture; dot with remaining ¼ cup fruit spread. Roll out remaining pastry to 10-inch circle. Cut into ½-inch wide strips. Form into lattice design over fruit. Combine egg yolk and sour cream; mix until well blended. Brush over pastry. Bake 10 minutes. *Reduce oven temperature to 350°F.* Continue baking 30 minutes or until pastry is golden brown and filling is hot and bubbly.* Cool on wire rack. Serve warm or at room temperature. *Makes 8 servings*

Pie may be covered loosely with foil during last 30 minutes of baking to prevent overbrowning, if desired.

Nutrients Per Serving:					
Calories	355	Carbohydrates	51g	Cholesterol	42mg
Protein	3g	Fat	16g	Sodium	283mg
Diabetic Exchanges Per Serving:					
1½ Starch/Bread, 3 Fat, 1¾ Fruit					

Strawberry Rhubarb Pie

BLUEBERRY PIE

**Cream Cheese Pastry
(recipe follows)
2 pints (4 cups) fresh *or*
thawed unsweetened
frozen blueberries
2 tablespoons cornstarch**

**⅔ cup no-sugar-added
blueberry preserves,
melted
¼ teaspoon ground nutmeg
1 egg yolk
1 tablespoon sour cream**

Preheat oven to 425°F. Prepare Cream Cheese Pastry. On lightly floured surface or pastry cloth, roll out half of dough to 11-inch circle. Place in 9-inch pie plate; set aside.

Combine blueberries and cornstarch in medium bowl; toss lightly to coat. Add preserves and nutmeg; mix lightly. Spoon into crust. Roll out remaining dough to 11-inch circle; place over fruit mixture. Turn edges under; flute. Cut several slits or circle in top crust to allow steam to escape. If desired, cut leaves from pastry scraps to decorate top of pie. Bake 10 minutes. Remove pie from oven. *Reduce oven temperature to 350°F.*

Combine egg yolk and sour cream; brush lightly over crust. Return pie to oven; continue baking 40 minutes or until crust is golden brown. Cool on wire rack. Serve warm, at room temperature or chilled.

Makes 8 servings

CREAM CHEESE PASTRY

**1½ cups all-purpose flour
½ cup cold butter or
margarine**

**3 ounces cream cheese,
cubed
1 teaspoon vanilla**

Place flour in large bowl. Cut in butter with pastry blender or two knives until mixture resembles coarse crumbs. Cut in cream cheese until mixture forms dough. Blend in vanilla.

Note: Pastry can be prepared in food processor with steel blade attached.

Nutrients Per Serving:					
Calories	342	Carbohydrates	45g	Cholesterol	70mg
Protein	4g	Fat	17g	Sodium	155mg
Diabetic Exchanges Per Serving:					
1½ Starch/Bread, 3¼ Fat, 1½ Fruit					

Blueberry Pie

FABULOUS FRUIT TART

Pastry for single-crust 9-inch pie

1 package (8 ounces) regular *or* reduced calorie cream cheese, softened

⅓ cup no-sugar-added raspberry fruit spread

½ cup sliced peaches *or* nectarines*

⅓ cup sliced strawberries*

½ cup kiwifruit slices*

⅓ cup raspberries*

3 tablespoons no-sugar-added apricot pourable fruit**

2 teaspoons raspberry-flavored liqueur (optional)

Preheat oven to 350°F. Roll out pastry to 12-inch circle; place in 10-inch tart pan with removable bottom or 10-inch quiche dish. Prick bottom and sides of pastry with fork. Bake 18 to 20 minutes or until golden brown. Cool completely on wire rack.

Combine cream cheese and fruit spread; mix well. Spread onto bottom of cooled pastry. Chill at least 1 hour. Just before serving, arrange fruit over cream cheese layer. Combine pourable fruit and liqueur, if desired; brush evenly over fruit. *Makes 8 servings*

Sliced bananas, plums or blueberries may be substituted.

**2 tablespoons no-sugar-added apricot fruit spread combined with 1 tablespoon warm water may be substituted.*

Nutrients Information Per Serving:					
Calories	274	Carbohydrates	26g	Cholesterol	38mg
Protein	3g	Fat	17g	Sodium	222mg
Diabetic Exchanges Per Serving:					
¾ Starch/Bread, 3½ Fat, 1 Fruit					

Fabulous Fruit Tart

EASY RASPBERRY CHIFFON PIE

**Pastry for single-crust
9-inch pie**
2 cups heavy cream
**6 ounces cream cheese,
softened**
2 teaspoons vanilla
**1 jar (10 ounces) no-sugar-
added raspberry fruit
spread (about 1 cup)**

**Fresh raspberries
(optional)**
**Fresh mint leaves
(optional)**

Preheat oven to 375°F. Roll out pastry to 11-inch circle; place in 9-inch pie plate. Trim and flute edges; prick bottom and sides of pastry with fork. Bake 15 minutes or until golden brown. Cool completely on wire rack.

Beat cream in small bowl at high speed with electric mixer until stiff peaks form; set aside. Combine cream cheese and vanilla in medium bowl; beat until light and fluffy. Blend in fruit spread, scraping sides of bowl frequently. Reserve ½ cup of the whipped cream for garnish; fold remaining whipped cream into cream cheese mixture until no white streaks remain. Spread evenly into cooled pie shell. Chill at least 2 hours or up to 24 hours. Just before serving, pipe or spoon reserved whipped cream around edge of pie. Garnish with raspberries and mint leaves, if desired.

Makes 8 servings

Nutrients Per Serving:					
Calories	475	Carbohydrates	33g	Cholesterol	112mg
Protein	4g	Fat	37g	Sodium	191mg

Diabetic Exchanges Per Serving:
¾ Starch/Bread, 7¼ Fat, 1½ Fruit

Easy Raspberry Chiffon Pie

LINZER TART

3/4 cup butter or margarine, softened
2 egg yolks
2 tablespoons thawed frozen unsweetened apple juice concentrate
2 teaspoons vanilla
1 cup all-purpose flour
1/2 teaspoon baking powder
1/4 teaspoon salt

1/4 teaspoon ground cinnamon
1/8 teaspoon ground allspice
1 1/2 cups ground blanched almonds *or* hazelnuts (about 8 ounces)
1 jar (10 ounces) no-sugar-added raspberry fruit spread (about 1 cup)

Beat butter in large bowl until light and fluffy. Blend in egg yolks, apple juice concentrate and vanilla. Combine flour, baking powder, salt, cinnamon and allspice; mix well. Stir in almonds. Gradually add to butter mixture, mixing until well blended. Spread 1 1/2 cups batter evenly onto bottom of 10-inch tart pan with removable bottom or 10-inch springform pan. Spread fruit spread evenly over batter, leaving 1-inch border around edge. Spoon remaining batter into pastry bag fitted with 1/2-inch plain or star tip. Pipe batter in lattice design over fruit spread. Chill 30 minutes.

Preheat oven to 350°F. Bake tart 35 minutes or until crust is golden brown and fruit spread is bubbly. Cool completely on wire rack. Serve at room temperature.

Makes 8 servings

Nutrients Per Serving:					
Calories	486	Carbohydrates	41g	Cholesterol	100mg
Protein	8g	Fat	34g	Sodium	276mg

Diabetic Exchanges Per Serving:
3/4 Starch/Bread, 1/2 Medium-Fat Meat, 6 1/4 Fat, 2 Fruit

Linzer Tart

APPLE-CHEDDAR TART

Cheddar Pastry (recipe follows)
1 egg white
6 cups peeled apple slices
2 teaspoons ground cinnamon
¼ teaspoon ground nutmeg
½ cup thawed frozen unsweeteened apple juice concentrate
2 tablespoons cornstarch
2 tablespoons butter or margarine
Sharp Cheddar cheese

Preheat oven to 400°F. Prepare Cheddar Pastry. Roll out pastry dough to 12-inch circle. Place in 10-inch tart pan with removable bottom or 10-inch quiche dish; trim pastry and flute edges, sealing to side of pan. Prick bottom and sides of pastry with fork. Beat egg white until frothy; brush lightly over bottom of pastry. Bake 15 minutes. *Reduce oven temperature to 350°F.*

Place apples in large bowl. Add cinnamon and nutmeg; toss lightly to coat. Combine apple juice concentrate and cornstarch; mix well. Add to apple mixture; mix lightly. Spoon into partially baked crust; dot with butter. Bake 35 to 40 minutes or until apples are tender and crust is golden brown. Cool on wire rack. Serve with sliced Cheddar cheese, if desired.

Makes 8 servings

CHEDDAR PASTRY

1½ cups all-purpose flour
⅓ cup (1½ ounces) shredded sharp Cheddar cheese
¼ teaspoon salt
½ cup cold butter or margarine
3 to 4 tablespoons ice water

Combine flour, cheese and salt in medium bowl. Cut in butter with pastry blender or two knives until mixture forms coarse crumbs. Add water, 1 tablespoon at a time, mixing just until mixture forms dough; wrap in plastic wrap. Refrigerate 1 hour.

Nutrients Per Serving:					
Calories	299	Carbohydrates	35g	Cholesterol	44mg
Protein	4g	Fat	16g	Sodium	255mg

Diabetic Exchanges Per Serving:
1 Starch/Bread, ¼ Medium-Fat Meat, 3 Fat, 1¼ Fruit

Apple-Cheddar Tart

FRESH STRAWBERRY–CREAM CHEESE TART

Pastry for single-crust 9-inch pie

8 ounces reduced-calorie *or* regular cream cheese, softened

¼ cup *plus* 1 tablespoon thawed frozen unsweetened pineapple juice concentrate, divided

1½ pints fresh strawberries,* hulled and halved (about 4 cups strawberry halves)

½ cup no-sugar-added strawberry fruit spread

Preheat oven to 350°F. Roll out pastry to 12-inch circle; place in 10-inch tart pan with removable bottom or 10-inch quiche dish. Trim edge of pastry ¼ inch above edge of tart pan to allow for shrinkage or flute decoratively in quiche dish. Prick bottom and sides of pastry with fork. Bake 12 to 15 minutes or until golden brown. Cool completely on wire rack.

Beat cream cheese with electric mixer or in food processor container until creamy. Gradually add ¼ cup pineapple juice concentrate, beating until smooth. Spread evenly over cooled pastry; top with strawberries. Combine fruit spread and remaining 1 tablespoon pineapple juice concentrate; mix well. Brush evenly over strawberries. Serve immediately or cover and refrigerate up to 2 hours before serving.

Makes 8 servings

*Do not use frozen strawberries

Nutrients Per Serving:					
Calories	263	Carbohydrates	35g	Cholesterol	22mg
Protein	4g	Fat	13g	Sodium	266mg
Diabetic Exchanges Per Serving:					
½ Starch/Bread, 2½ Fat, 1¾ Fruit					

SPICED PEACH PIE

Pastry for double-crust
9-inch pie
1 egg, separated
5 cups peeled sliced fresh
peaches *or* frozen
unsweetened sliced
peaches, thawed and
well drained
2 tablespoons cornstarch
2 teaspoons ground
cinnamon
½ teaspoon ground nutmeg
⅛ teaspoon salt
½ cup thawed frozen
unsweeteened apple
juice concentrate
1 teaspoon vanilla
1 tablespoon butter or
margarine
1 teaspoon cold water

Preheat oven to 400°F. Roll out half of pastry to 11-inch circle. Place in 9-inch pie plate. Beat egg white until frothy; brush lightly onto bottom of pastry. Set aside. Place peaches in large bowl. Combine cornstarch, cinnamon, nutmeg and salt; mix well. Blend in apple juice concentrate and vanilla. Pour over peaches; toss lightly to coat. Spoon into pie shell; dot with butter. Cut remaining pastry into ½-inch wide strips; form into lattice design over peaches. Beat together egg yolk and water; brush lightly over pastry. Bake 50 minutes or until pastry is golden brown and filling is hot and bubbly.* Cool on wire rack. Serve warm, at room temperature or chilled.   *Makes 8 servings*

Pie may be covered loosely with foil after 30 minutes of baking to prevent overbrowing, if desired.

Nutrients Per Serving:					
Calories	345	Carbohydrates	45g	Cholesterol	45mg
Protein	3g	Fat	17g	Sodium	272mg

Diabetic Exchanges Per Serving:
1¾ Starch/Bread, 3¼ Fat, 1¼ Fruit

Divine Desserts

RASPBERRY–PEAR DUMPLINGS

**Pastry for double crust
  pie***
1 egg white, beaten
4 small firm ripe pears

**¼ cup no-sugar-added
  raspberry fruit spread**
1 egg yolk
1 tablespoon sour cream

Preheat oven to 350°F. Roll pastry on lightly floured surface to ⅛-inch thickness. Cut four squares, each 6 inches square or large enough to enclose one pear; brush with egg white. Let stand 10 minutes. Meanwhile, peel pears. Hollow out core of each pear to within ½ inch of bottom; fill with fruit spread. Place one pear on each pastry square; bring up four corners, pressing points together at top of pear to seal, using small amount of water to moisten pastry, if necessary. If desired, cut leaves from pastry scraps to decorate top of dumplings. Place in shallow baking dish. Beat egg yolk with sour cream; brush over dumplings. Bake 40 minutes or until pastry is golden brown and pears are tender when pierced with sharp knife. Serve warm or at room temperature. *Makes 4 servings*

Or use Cream Cheese Pastry from Blueberry Pie (page 48).

Nutrients Per Serving:

Calories	615	Carbohydrates	77g	Cholesterol	85mg
Protein	6g	Fat	32g	Sodium	438mg

Diabetic Exchanges Per Serving:
2½ Starch/Bread, 6¼ Fat, 2½ Fruit

Raspberry-Pear Dumplings

CREAMY STRAWBERRY BLINTZES

Crêpes (recipe follows)
4 ounces cream cheese, softened
1½ teaspoons vanilla
1 cup part-skim ricotta cheese
1½ cups chopped fresh *or* unsweetened frozen strawberries (do not thaw)

½ cup *plus* 2 tablespoons no-sugar-added strawberry fruit spread
Strawberry halves (optional)
Sour cream or crème fraîche (optional)
Fresh mint leaves (optional)

Prepare Crêpes; set aside. Preheat oven to 350°F. Place cream cheese and vanilla in food processor or blender container; cover and process until smooth. Add ricotta cheese; process until smooth. Stir in chopped strawberries. Spoon 2 heaping tablespoons filling down center of each crêpe; roll up. Place seam side down in lightly oiled or buttered 12 × 8-inch baking dish. Bake 15 to 18 minutes or until thoroughly heated. Serve warm with fruit spread. Top with strawberry halves and garnish with sour cream and mint leaves, if desired.

Makes 5 servings

CRÊPES

¾ cup all-purpose flour
¾ cup milk
2 eggs

1 tablespoon butter or margarine

Combine flour, milk, eggs and butter in food processor or blender container; cover and process until smooth. Let stand at room temperature 1 hour or cover and refrigerate up to 8 hours. Process to combine again just before cooking crêpes. Heat 5- or 6-inch crêpe pan over medium heat; lightly brush with oil or melted butter. Pour scant ¼ cup batter into hot pan all at once, tilting and rotating pan to spread batter evenly. Cook until bottom of crêpe is lightly browned; turn over. Continue cooking 30 seconds. Remove each crêpe to separate sheet of waxed paper. Repeat with remaining batter.

Makes 10 crêpes

Nutrients Per Serving:

Calories	390	Carbohydrates	44g	Cholesterol	137mg
Protein	13g	Fat	18g	Sodium	196mg

Diabetic Exchanges Per Serving:
1 Starch/Bread; ¼ Dairy, Skim Milk; 1 Medium-Fat Meat; 2½ Fat; 1¾ Fruit

Creamy Strawberry Blintzes

PEACHES & CINNAMON RICE PUDDING

1 cup water
⅓ cup uncooked rice (*not* converted)
1 tablespoon butter or margarine
⅛ teaspoon salt
1 can (16 ounces) sliced peaches in unsweetened juice, undrained
½ cup milk, divided
2 teaspoons cornstarch
½ teaspoon ground cinnamon
¼ cup no-sugar-added peach fruit spread
½ cup heavy cream (optional)
1 tablespoon no-sugar-added peach fruit spread (optional)
Fresh peach slices (optional)
Cinnamon sticks (optional)

Combine water, rice, butter and salt in medium saucepan. Bring to a boil over high heat. Reduce heat to low. Cover; simmer until rice is tender, about 25 minutes. Remove from heat. Drain canned peaches, reserving ½ cup juice; set peaches aside. Add reserved juice and ¼ cup milk to rice; set aside. Combine cornstarch and cinnamon; mix well. Gradually add remaining ¼ cup milk, stirring until smooth. Add to rice mixture; return to heat. Bring to a boil over medium-high heat, stirring constantly. Reduce heat to low. Simmer, stirring frequently, until thickened, about 2 minutes. Remove from heat; stir in ¼ cup fruit spread. Cool to room temperature, stirring occasionally. Chop drained peaches; stir into pudding. Serve at room temperature or chilled. If desired, beat cream and 1 tablespoon fruit spread until soft peaks form. Serve with pudding. Garnish with fresh peach slices and cinnamon sticks, if desired. *Makes 4 servings*

Nutrients Per Serving:					
Calories	197	Carbohydrates	39g	Cholesterol	12mg
Protein	3g	Fat	4g	Sodium	119mg

Diabetic Exchanges Per Serving:
¾ Starch/Bread, ¾ Fat, 1¾ Fruit

Peaches & Cinnamon Rice Pudding

GERMAN APPLE PANCAKE

¼ cup butter or margarine
1½ teaspoons ground
    cinnamon, divided
2 large cooking apples,*
    peeled and thinly sliced
    (about 3 cups)
3 eggs, beaten
½ cup thawed frozen
    unsweetened apple
    juice concentrate

½ cup all-purpose flour
¼ cup half-and-half *or* heavy
    cream
1 teaspoon vanilla
¼ teaspoon ground nutmeg
⅛ teaspoon salt
    Apple Cream (recipe
    follows)

Preheat oven to 450°F. Melt butter with ½ teaspoon cinnamon in 9- or 10-inch ovenproof skillet.** Add apples; cook and stir until tender, about 4 minutes. Place eggs, apple juice concentrate, flour, half-and-half, vanilla, remaining 1 teaspoon cinnamon, nutmeg and salt in food processor container; cover and process until smooth. Pour over apples. Bake 10 minutes or until pancake is set in center. Cut into wedges. Serve warm or at room temperature with Apple Cream.

Makes 6 servings

Use Jonathon, Rome Beauty or McIntosh.

**If ovenproof skillet is unavailable, use regular skillet. Cook apple mixture as directed; spoon into 9-inch pie plate. Continue as directed.*

APPLE CREAM

½ cup plain yogurt
2 tablespoons thawed
    frozen unsweetened
    apple juice concentrate

½ teaspoon vanilla

Combine all ingredients; mix until well blended.

Nutrients Per Serving:					
Calories	256	Carbohydrates	32g	Cholesterol	132mg
Protein	6g	Fat	12g	Sodium	181mg

Diabetic Exchanges Per Serving:
½ Starch/Bread, ½ Medium-Fat Meat, 2 Fat, 1½ Fruit

German Apple Pancake

STRAWBERRY–BANANA GRANITÉ

2 ripe medium bananas, peeled and sliced (about 2 cups)

2 cups unsweetened frozen strawberries (do not thaw)

¼ cup no-sugar-added strawberry pourable fruit*

Whole fresh strawberries (optional)

Fresh mint leaves (optional)

Place banana slices in plastic bag; freeze until firm. Place frozen banana slices and frozen strawberries in food processor container. Let stand 10 minutes for fruit to soften slightly. Add pourable fruit. Remove plunger from top of food processor to allow air to be incorporated. Process until smooth, scraping down sides of container frequently. Serve immediately. Garnish with fresh strawberries and mint leaves, if desired. Freeze leftovers. *Makes 5 servings*

3 tablespoons no-sugar-added strawberry fruit spread combined with 1 tablespoon warm water may be substitiuted.

Note: Granité may be transferred to airtight container and frozen up to 1 month. Let stand at room temperature 10 minutes to soften slightly before serving.

Nutrients Per Serving:					
Calories	77	Carbohydrates	20g	Cholesterol	0mg
Protein	1g	Fat	tr	Sodium	8mg
Diabetic Exchanges Per Serving:					
1¼ Fruit					

BANANAS FLAMBÉ

2 tablespoons butter or margarine

½ teaspoon ground cinnamon

2 small firm ripe bananas, peeled and cut in half lengthwise

2 tablespoons thawed frozen unsweetened apple juice concentrate

2 tablespoons brandy *or* cognac

continued on page 70

Strawberry-Banana Granité

Melt butter in 10-inch skillet over medium heat. Stir in cinnamon. Add bananas; cook until thoroughly heated, about 1 minute per side. Add apple juice concentrate; cook 1 minute, stirring occasionally. Drizzle with brandy; remove from heat. Carefully ignite with lighted match. Carefully shake skillet until flames are extinguished. Transfer bananas to individual dessert dishes, reserving liquid in skillet. Cook liquid over medium-high heat until thickened and bubbly, about 1 minute. Pour over bananas; serve immediately. *Makes 2 servings*

Nutrients Per Serving:					
Calories	234	Carbohydrates	29g	Cholesterol	31mg
Protein	1g	Fat	12g	Sodium	123mg
Diabetic Exchanges Per Serving:					
2½ Fat, 2 Fruit					

POACHED DRIED FRUIT COMPOTE

8 ounces mixed dried fruit, such as apricots, pears, apples and prunes
1½ cups water

½ cup white Riesling *or* Rhine wine*
2 cinnamon sticks
4 whole cloves

Combine all ingredients in medium saucepan. Bring to a boil over high heat. Reduce heat to low; simmer, uncovered, 12 to 15 minutes or until fruit is tender. Cool. Discard cinnamon sticks and cloves. Serve warm, at room temperature or chilled in individual dessert bowls. Garnish with additional cinnamon sticks, if desired.
Makes 6 servings

White grape juice may be substituted.

Nutrients Per Serving:					
Calories	106	Carbohydrates	25g	Cholesterol	0mg
Protein	1g	Fat	tr	Sodium	8mg
Diabetic Exchanges Per Serving:					
1¾ Fruit					

Poached Dried Fruit Compote

WATERMELON ICE

4 cups seeded 1-inch
  watermelon chunks
¼ cup thawed frozen
  unsweetened pineapple
  juice concentrate

2 tablespoons fresh lime
  juice
Fresh melon balls
  (optional)
Fresh mint leaves
  (optional)

Place melon chunks in single layer in plastic freezer bag; freeze until firm, about 8 hours. Place frozen melon in food processor container fitted with steel blade. Let stand 15 minutes to soften slightly. Add pineapple juice and lime juice. Remove plunger from top of food processor to allow air to be incorporated. Process until smooth, scraping down sides of container frequently. Spoon into individual dessert dishes. Garnish with melon balls and mint leaves, if desired. Freeze leftovers.

Makes 6 servings

Honeydew Ice: Substitute honeydew for the watermelon and unsweetened pineapple-guava-orange juice concentrate for the pineapple juice concentrate.

Cantaloupe Ice: Substitute cantaloupe for the watermelon and unsweetened pineapple-guava-orange juice concentrate for the pineapple juice concentrate.

Note: Ices may be transferred to airtight container and frozen up to 1 month. Let stand at room temperature 10 minutes to soften slightly before serving.

Nutrients Per Serving:					
Calories	57	Carbohydrates	13g	Cholesterol	0mg
Protein	1g	Fat	tr	Sodium	3mg
Diabetic Exchanges Per Serving:					
1 Fruit					

Clockwise from top: Honeydew Ice, Cantaloupe Ice
and Watermelon Ice

CRÊPES SUZETTE

**1 recipe Crêpes* (see Creamy
    Strawberry Blintzes,
    page 62)
No-sugar-added orange
    marmalade *or*
    pineapple fruit spread**

**Butter or margarine
Orange-flavored liqueur**

Prepare Crêpes; cool to room temperature. For each serving of Crêpes Suzette, spread one side of *each* of two crepes with 1½ tablespoons marmalade; fold in half. (Any remaining crepes may be wrapped in single sheets of waxed paper, placed in freezer-weight plastic bag and frozen up to 3 months.) For *each* two filled crepes, melt 1 tablespoon butter in 10-inch skillet over medium heat. Add crepes; cook 2 minutes. Turn over; continue cooking 1 minute. Drizzle with 2 tablespoons liqueur; remove from heat. Carefully ignite with lighted match. Carefully shake skillet until flames are extinguished. Transfer crepes to warm serving plate; top with liquid from skillet. Serve immediately.

*One recipe of 10 crêpes will yield 5 servings Crêpes Suzette.

Nutrients Per Serving:					
Calories	428	Carbohydrates	57g	Cholesterol	127mg
Protein	6g	Fat	17g	Sodium	184mg

Diabetic Exchanges Per Serving:
1 Starch/Bread, ½ Medium-Fat Meat, 3 Fat, 2¾ Fruit

BAKED APPLE CUSTARD

**1½ cups unsweetened
    applesauce
1 teaspoon ground
    cinnamon
¼ teaspoon salt
½ cup half-and-half
¼ cup thawed frozen
    unsweetened apple
    juice concentrate**

**4 eggs, beaten
½ teaspoon ground nutmeg
   Additional half-and-half
   (optional)**

Preheat oven to 350°F. Combine applesauce, cinnamon and salt in large bowl. Blend in half-and-half, apple juice concentrate and eggs. Pour into shallow 1½-quart or 8-inch square baking dish. Place dish in larger baking pan or shallow roasting pan. Add enough hot water to roasting pan to come 1 inch up sides of baking dish. Sprinkle custard with nutmeg. Bake 45 minutes or until knife inserted near center of custard comes out clean. Cool completely on wire rack; chill. Spoon into individual dessert dishes. Serve with half-and-half, if desired. *Makes 6 servings*

Nutrients Per Serving:

Calories	123	Carbohydrates	13g	Cholesterol	149mg
Protein	5g	Fat	6g	Sodium	145mg

Diabetic Exchanges Per Serving:
¾ Medium-Fat Meat, ¼ Fat, 1 Fruit

FRUIT MOUSSE

1 cup heavy cream
1 teaspoon vanilla
1 package (3 ounces) cream cheese, softened

½ cup no-sugar-added strawberry *or* seedless raspberry fruit spread

Combine cream and vanilla in small bowl of electric mixer; beat at high speed until stiff peaks form. Transfer to separate bowl. In same small mixer bowl, beat cream cheese until creamy. Blend in fruit spread. Fold in whipped cream mixture. Spoon into individual dessert dishes; chill at least 2 hours or up to 24 hours before serving. *Makes 6 servings*

Variation: Layer mousse with unsweetened fresh sliced strawberries or raspberries in parfait glasses; chill up to 4 hours before serving.

Nutrients Per Serving:

Calories	245	Carbohydrates	16g	Cholesterol	70mg
Protein	2g	Fat	20g	Sodium	57mg

Diabetic Exchanges Per Serving:
4 Fat, 1 Fruit

SUMMER FRUIT CLAFOUTI
(Custard Puff)

1½ cups sliced ripe peaches, nectarines *or* plums*
⅔ cup half-and-half
¼ cup no-sugar-added peach fruit spread
2 eggs
2 tablespoons all-purpose flour
2 tablespoons butter or margarine, melted

1 teaspoon vanilla
¼ teaspoon ground nutmeg
⅛ teaspoon salt
Peachy Topping (recipe follows)
Additional ground nutmeg (optional)

Preheat oven to 375°F. Lightly grease 9-inch glass pie plate. Place fruit in pinwheel-fashion in pie plate. Place all remaining ingredients *except* Peachy Topping and additional nutmeg in food processor container fitted with steel blade; cover and process until smooth, about 20 seconds. Pour over fruit. Bake 35 minutes or until puffed and golden brown. (Clafouti will fall upon cooling). Serve warm, at room temperature or chilled with Peachy Topping. Sprinkle with additional nutmeg, if desired. *Makes 6 servings*

1 can (16 ounces) sliced peaches in unsweetened juice, well drained, may be substituted.

PEACHY TOPPING

¼ cup sour cream *or* crème fraîche

2 tablespoons no-sugar-added peach fruit

Combine ingredients; mix until well blended.

Nutrients Per Serving:					
Calories	187	Carbohydrates	19g	Cholesterol	95mg
Protein	4g	Fat	11g	Sodium	122mg
Diabetic Exchanges Per Serving:					
½ Medium-Fat Meat, 1½ Fat, 1¼ Fruit					

Summer Fruit Clafouti

QUICK "BAKED" APPLES

4 cooking apples*
2 tablespoons chopped raisins
2 tablespoons chopped dates
2 tablespoons chopped walnuts *or* pecans
1 tablespoon butter or margarine, melted

1 teaspoon cornstarch
¾ teaspoon ground cinnamon
¾ cup thawed frozen unsweetened apple juice concentrate
Sour cream or crème fraîche (optional)

Microwave: Remove peel from top and halfway down sides of each apple, starting at stem end. With apple corer or sharp knife, remove core to within ¼ inch of bottom of apple, leaving bottom stem end intact. Place apples in 9-inch microwavable pie plate or shallow baking dish. Combine raisins, dates, walnuts and butter; spoon into center of apples. Combine cornstarch and cinnamon. Blend in apple juice concentrate; drizzle over apples. Microwave, uncovered, on HIGH 10 to 12 minutes or until apples are tender when pierced with sharp knife, rotating dish every 6 minutes. Let stand 5 to 10 minutes before serving. Spoon juices from dish over apples. Serve warm or at room temperature with sour cream, if desired.   *Makes 4 servings*

**Use Jonathon, McIntosh or Rome Beauty apples.*

Note: For 2 servings, cut all ingredients in half. Peel, core and fill apples as directed. Place in 9-inch microwavable pie plate or shallow baking dish. Microwave on HIGH 5 to 8 minutes or until tender when pierced with sharp knife, rotating dish after 4 minutes. Continue as directed.

Nutrients Per Serving:

Calories	251	Carbohydrates	52g	Cholesterol	8mg
Protein	1g	Fat	6g	Sodium	44mg

Diabetic Exchanges Per Serving:
1 Fat, 3½ Fruit

FRUIT SOUP

¾ cup part-skim ricotta
cheese
¼ cup heavy cream *or* half-
and-half
1 cup thawed frozen
unsweetened
strawberries,
undrained, *or* 1 cup
crushed fresh
strawberries

⅓ cup no-sugar-added
strawberry pourable
fruit*
¼ cup dry red wine
(optional)
Sour cream (optional)
Sliced fresh strawberries
(optional)
Fresh mint leaves
(optional)

Place ricotta cheese in blender container; blend until smooth. Blend in cream, strawberries, pourable fruit and wine. Chill at least 2 hours or up to 8 hours. Serve garnished with sour cream, sliced strawberries and mint leaves, if desired.   *Makes 2 servings*

*3 tablespoons no-sugar-added strawberry fruit spread combined with 2 tablespoons warm water may be substitiuted.

Nutrients Per Serving:					
Calories	352	Carbohydrates	36g	Cholesterol	69mg
Protein	11g	Fat	18g	Sodium	161mg
Diabetic Exchanges Per Serving:					
1½ Medium-Fat Meat, 2 Fat, 2½ Fruit					

BANANA–ORANGE SAUCE

1 ripe medium banana
3 tablespoons orange juice
1 tablespoon orange-
flavored liqueur
(optional)

¼ teaspoon grated orange
peel
Dash of ground nutmeg

Peel banana; cut into chunks. Place in blender container with remaining ingredients; blend until smooth. Serve immediately over fresh fruit, granité or snack cake.   *Makes ½ cup*

Nutrients Per Tablespoon:					
Calories	16	Carbohydrates	4g	Cholesterol	0mg
Protein	tr	Fat	tr	Sodium	tr
Diabetic Exchanges Per Tablespoon:					
¼ Fruit					

Fruit Soup

PROFITEROLES WITH APRICOT PASTRY CREAM
(Miniature Cream Puffs with Apricot Pastry Cream)

1 cup all-purpose flour	**Apricot Pastry Cream**
⅛ teaspoon salt	**(recipe follows)**
1 cup water	**Raspberry Coulis Dessert**
⅓ cup butter or margarine	**Sauce (page 84),**
1 teaspoon vanilla	**optional**
4 eggs, at room temperature	**Fresh raspberry leaves**
	(optional)

Preheat oven to 400°F. Combine flour and salt; set aside. Bring water and butter to a boil in heavy medium saucepan over medium-high heat. Add flour mixture all at once; beat vigorously until dough leaves sides of pan and forms a smooth ball. Remove from heat; let stand 2 minutes. Beat in vanilla. Beat in eggs, one at a time. Drop heaping tablespoonfuls of dough, 2 inches apart, onto lightly greased cookie sheets. Bake 10 minutes. *Reduce oven temperature to 350°F.* Continue baking 25 minutes or until golden brown. (*Do not open oven door during baking.*) Cool completely on wire racks.

Just before serving, prepare Apricot Pastry Cream. Cut cream puffs in half horizontally with serrated knife. Remove soft dough from center of puffs; discard. Fill puffs with pastry cream; replace tops. Serve with Raspberry Dessert Sauce and garnish with fresh raspberry leaves, if desired.   *Makes 6 servings (18 profiteroles)*

APRICOT PASTRY CREAM

½ cup heavy cream	**½ cup no-sugar-added**
6 ounces whipped cream	**apricot fruit spread**
cheese	

Beat cream at high speed in small bowl of electric mixer until soft peaks form. Combine cream cheese and fruit spread in medium bowl; mix until well blended. Fold in whipped cream.

Note: Profiteroles may be filled and refrigerated up to 2 hours before serving.

Nutrients Per Serving:					
Calories	442	Carbohydrates	33g	Cholesterol	226mg
Protein	9g	Fat	31g	Sodium	309mg

Diabetic Exchanges Per Serving:
1 Starch/Bread, ¾ Lean Meat, 5½ Fat, 1 Fruit

Profiteroles with Apricot Pastry Cream

RASPBERRY–COULIS DESSERT SAUCE

2 cups (1 pint) fresh *or*
    thawed frozen
    unsweetened
    raspberries
½ cup no-sugar-added
    seedless raspberry fruit
    spread

1½ tablespoons orange-
    flavored liqueur
    (optional)

Place raspberries in blender or food processor container; cover and blend until smooth. Strain; discard seeds. Combine purée, fruit spread and liqueur, if desired; mix well. Store in refrigerator up to 1 week. Serve over fresh fruit or cake slices.

Makes 1 cup

Nutrients Per Tablespoon:					
Calories	29	Carbohydrates	7g	Cholesterol	0mg
Protein	tr	Fat	tr	Sodium	0mg
Diabetic Exchanges Per Tablespoon:					
½ Fruit					

APRICOT DESSERT SOUFFLÉ

3 tablespoons butter
2 tablespoons all-purpose
    flour
1 cup no-sugar-added
    apricot pourable fruit*
⅓ cup finely chopped dried
    apricots
3 tablespoons apricot
    brandy (optional)

3 egg yolks, beaten
4 egg whites
¼ teaspoon cream of tartar
⅛ teaspoon salt
    Unsweetened whipped
    cream (optional)

Preheat oven to 325°F. Melt butter in medium saucepan. Add flour; cook, stirring constantly, until bubbly. Add pourable fruit and apricots; cook, stirring constantly, until thickened, about 3 minutes. Remove from heat; blend in egg yolks and brandy, if desired. Cool to room temperature, stirring occasionally. Beat egg whites with cream of tartar and salt at high speed in small bowl of electric mixer until stiff peaks form. Gently fold into apricot mixture. Spoon into 1½-quart soufflé dish. Bake 30 minutes or until puffed and golden brown.** Serve immediately with whipped cream, if desired.

Makes 6 servings

*³⁄₄ *cup no-sugar-added fruit spread mixed with ¼ cup warm water may be substituted.*

****Soufflé will be soft in center. For a firmer soufflé, increase baking time to 35 minutes.*

Nutrients Per Serving:					
Calories	214	Carbohydrates	31g	Cholesterol	122mg
Protein	4g	Fat	8g	Sodium	179mg
Diabetic Exchanges Per Serving:					
½ Medium-Fat Meat, 1¼ Fat, 2 Fruit					

FROZEN PEANUT BUTTER–BANANA DESSERT

2 large ripe bananas, cut into ½-inch slices
½ cup no-sugar-added natural peanut butter (creamy *or* chunky)

½ cup half-and-half

Place bananas in single layer in plastic freezer bag; freeze until firm, at least 8 hours. Combine peanut butter and half-and-half in food processor container fitted with steel blade; cover and process until smooth. Add frozen bananas; let stand 10 minutes to soften slightly. Process until smooth, scraping down sides of container frequently. (Dessert will be soft-set.) Serve immediately or cover and freeze in airtight container until serving time. Freeze leftovers.

Makes 4 servings

Note: Place frozen dessert in refrigerator 15 to 20 minutes before serving or let stand at room temperature 10 minutes before serving to soften slightly.

Nutrients Per Serving:					
Calories	299	Carbohydrates	23g	Cholesterol	11mg
Protein	10g	Fat	20g	Sodium	138mg
Diabetic Exchanges Per Serving:					
½ Starch/Bread, 1 High-Fat Meat, 2½ Fat, 1 Fruit					

FRUIT & CHEESE CRISPS

½ cup part-skim ricotta
cheese
1 tablespoon almond-
flavored liqueur *or*
thawed frozen
unsweetened apple
juice concentrate *plus*
¼ teaspoon almond
extract
¼ cup toasted slivered
almonds

4 no-sugar-added
crispbread *or*
crackerbread
rectangles,* any flavor
¼ cup sliced fresh
strawberries
¼ cup sliced fresh peaches
No-sugar-added
strawberry *or* raspberry
pourable fruit
(optional)

Combine ricotta cheese and liqueur; mix well. Stir in almonds; spread
evenly over crispbread. Top with fruit. Brush with pourable fruit, if
desired; serve immediately. Garnish with mint leaves, if desired.

Makes 4 servings

8 crispbread squares may be substituted for 4 crispbread rectangles.

Nutrients Per Serving:					
Calories	135	Carbohydrates	11g	Cholesterol	10mg
Protein	6g	Fat	7g	Sodium	79mg
Diabetic Exchanges Per Serving:					
1 Medium-Fat Meat, ¼ Fat, ¾ Fruit					

PECAN–RAISIN BREAD PUDDING

½ of a 1-pound loaf day-old
French bread,* sliced
¾ inch thick
4 tablespoons butter or
margarine, divided
¾ cup golden *or* dark raisins
3 eggs, beaten
1 cup thawed frozen
unsweetened apple
juice concentrate

2 cups half-and-half
1 tablespoon vanilla
½ teaspoon ground
cinnamon
¼ teaspoon ground nutmeg
¼ teaspoon salt
½ cup coarsely chopped
pecans
No-sugar-added pourable
fruit (optional)

continued on page 88

Fruit & Cheese Crisps

Pecan-Raisin Bread Pudding, continued

Toast bread slices; spread with 2 tablespoons butter. Cut into ¾-inch pieces. Brush 1 tablespoon butter onto bottom and sides of shallow 1½-quart baking dish. Add bread and raisins; mix lightly. Combine eggs, apple juice concentrate, half-and-half, vanilla, cinnamon, nutmeg and salt; mix until well blended. Pour over bread mixture; press down bread pieces to saturate. Let stand 20 minutes.

Preheat oven to 375°F. Place baking dish in larger shallow baking pan or roasting pan; add enough hot water to baking pan to come 1 inch up sides of casserole. Bake 30 minutes. Melt remaining 1 tablespoon butter. Add pecans; toss lightly to coat. Sprinkle over pudding. Continue baking 8 to 10 minutes or until pecans are toasted and pudding is set. Cool on wire rack. Serve warm or at room temperature with pourable fruit, if desired.   *Makes 6 servings*

*Sour dough bread, Italian bread or one French bread baguette may be substituted.

Nutrients Per Serving:					
Calories	520	Carbohydrates	61g	Cholesterol	158mg
Protein	11g	Fat	27g	Sodium	466mg
Diabetic Exchanges Per Serving:					
1½ Starch/Bread, ¾ Medium-Fat Meat, 4 Fat, 2½ Fruit					

GINGERED PEACH SAUCE

**1 can (16 ounces) sliced
 peaches in unsweetened
 juice, drained
1½ teaspoons minced fresh
 ginger**

**2 tablespoons almond-
 flavored liqueur
 (optional)**

Place peaches in food processor container fitted with steel blade; cover and process until smooth, scraping down sides of container once. Add ginger and liqueur, if desired; process until smooth. Serve with fresh fruit.   *Makes about 1 cup*

Nutrients Per Tablespoon:					
Calories	13	Carbohydrates	3g	Cholesterol	0mg
Protein	tr	Fat	0g	Sodium	1mg
Diabetic Exchanges Per Tablespoon:					
¼ Fruit					

Gingered Peach Sauce

BERRY COBBLER

1 pint fresh raspberries
   (2½ cups)*
1 pint fresh blueberries *or*
   strawberries, sliced
   (2½ cups)*
2 tablespoons cornstarch
½ cup no-sugar-added
   raspberry pourable
   fruit**
1 cup all-purpose flour

1½ teaspoons baking powder
¼ teaspoon salt
⅓ cup milk
⅓ cup butter or margarine,
   melted
2 tablespoons thawed
   frozen unsweetened
   apple juice concentrate
¼ teaspoon ground nutmeg

Preheat oven to 375°F. Combine berries and cornstarch in medium
bowl; toss lightly to coat. Add pourable fruit; mix well. Spoon into
1½-quart or 8-inch square baking dish. Combine flour, baking powder
and salt in medium bowl. Add milk, butter and concentrate; mix just
until dry ingredients are moistened. Drop six heaping tablespoonfuls
of batter evenly over berries; sprinkle with nutmeg. Bake 25 minutes
or until topping is golden brown and fruit is bubbly. Cool on wire
rack. Serve warm or at room temperature.   *Makes 6 servings*

*One (16-ounce) bag frozen raspberries and one (16-ounce) bag
frozen blueberries or strawberries may be substituted for fresh berries.
Thaw berries, reserving juices. Increase cornstarch to 3 tablespoons.*

***⅓ cup raspberry fruit spread combined with 3 tablespoons warm
water may be substituted.*

Nutrients Per Serving:					
Calories	302	Carbohydrates	48g	Cholesterol	29mg
Protein	4g	Fat	11g	Sodium	329mg

Diabetic Exchanges Per Serving:
1 Starch/Bread, 2¼ Fat, 2 Fruit

Berry Cobbler

APPLE–RAISIN CRISP

1 cup *plus* 3 tablespoons thawed frozen unsweetened apple juice concentrate, divided
¼ cup uncooked rolled oats
4 large cooking apples,* peeled, cored and sliced (about 6 cups sliced)
¾ cup raisins
2 tablespoons cornstarch
2 teaspoons ground cinnamon, divided
½ teaspoon ground nutmeg
¼ teaspoon salt
½ cup all-purpose flour
¼ cup cold butter or margarine
½ cup chopped walnuts *or* pecans (optional)
Unsweetened whipped cream (optional)

Preheat oven to 375°F. Combine 3 tablespoons apple juice concentrate and oats; mix lightly. Set aside. Combine apples and raisins in large bowl; set aside. Combine cornstarch, 1½ teaspoons cinnamon, nutmeg and salt in medium bowl; mix well. Blend in remaining 1 cup apple juice concentrate. Add to apple mixture; mix lightly to coat. Spoon into shallow 1½-quart or 8-inch square baking dish. Combine flour and remaining ½ teaspoon cinnamon; cut in butter with pastry blender or two knives until mixture resembles coarse crumbs. Add oat mixture; mix lightly. Stir in walnuts, if desired; sprinkle evenly over apple mixture. Bake 35 minutes or until apples are tender. Serve warm, at room temperature or chilled with whipped cream, if desired.   *Makes 6 servings*

Use Jonathan, Rome Beauty, Courtland or McIntosh apples.

Nutrients Per Serving:					
Calories	341	Carbohydrates	67g	Cholesterol	21mg
Protein	3g	Fat	9g	Sodium	185mg

Diabetic Exchanges Per Serving:
¾ Starch/Bread, 1¾ Fat, 3¾ Fruit

Apple-Raisin Crisp

RICOTTA CHEESE DESSERT PANCAKES

⅓ cup part-skim ricotta
   cheese
¼ cup milk
1 egg
2 tablespoons thawed
   frozen unsweetened
   apple juice concentrate
1 tablespoon butter or
   margarine, melted

¾ teaspoon vanilla
½ cup all-purpose flour
½ teaspoon baking powder
⅛ teaspoon ground nutmeg
1 cup *plus* 2 tablespoons
   no-sugar-added
   pourable fruit,* any
   flavor

Preheat lightly oiled griddle or skillet over medium heat. Place ricotta cheese in food processor container fitted with steel blade; cover and process until smooth. Add milk, egg, apple juice concentrate, butter and vanilla; process until blended. Add flour, baking powder and nutmeg; pulse just until dry ingredients are moistened. Drop heaping tablespoonfuls of batter, 4 inches apart, onto prepared griddle. Cook 1 to 2 minutes or until bubbles appear on surface; turn over. Continue cooking until lightly browned, about 30 seconds. Serve warm with pourable fruit.   *Makes about 6 servings (18 pancakes)*

*¾ cup no-sugar-added fruit spread combined with 6 tablespoons warm water may be substituted.

Nutrients Per Serving:

Calories	212	Carbohydrates	39g	Cholesterol	46mg
Protein	4g	Fat	4g	Sodium	126mg

Diabetic Exchanges Per Serving:
½ Starch/Bread, ⅓ Medium-Fat Meat, ½ Fat, 2 Fruit

Index

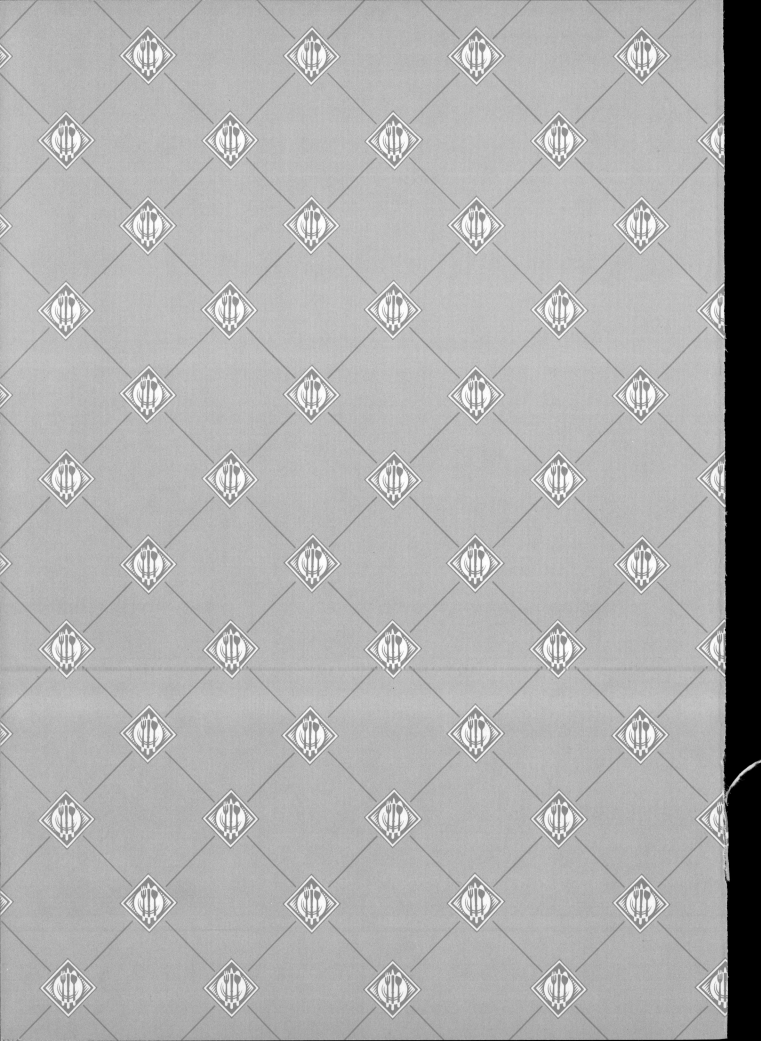